This year we are invited to think about – and pray for – a *Calm and Bright* Christmas for ourselves, our communities and our world. What might this mean for us, when suffering, pain and darkness can feel overwhelming?

The world of the wise men wasn't so different from our world today – they knew poverty, danger, armed conflict and power-hungry rulers.

And yet, the angels urged Mary, Joseph and the shepherds not to be afraid, but to trust in the good news of God's love. The most common command in the Old Testament is 'do not fear' – a command virtually always followed by, 'for I am with you'.

Finding moments of 'calm and bright' does not mean we deny, minimise or ignore the storms we face. Rather, we see that God is in the midst.

As we remember the wise men gathering around the Christ-child, we celebrate God is still with us, whatever storms might be raging in the world and in our lives.

Our prayer is that all of us – whatever lies behind or ahead – may find this moment of hope-filled and joyful calm as we worship together this Christmas.

Archbishop Justin Welby
Archbishop Stephen Cottrell

CW00566382

Introduction

December can feel like chaos – full of social events, services, Christmas presents to buy, never-ending to-do lists and the pressure to create the perfect Christmas.

Amid the challenges of a fast-moving and busy culture, it can sometimes be difficult to find moments where we can rest and simply be – especially with the added complexities that Christmas brings.

This year, we invite you to join with us over twelve days reflecting on words from the well-known carol:

"Silent Night! Holy Night!
All is calm, all is bright ..."

Journey with us as we dwell in the still centre of the Christmas story. We will meet shepherds and angels along the way, finding those moments of calm and contemplation as Mary did that first Christmas, as well as embracing the joy and gentleness of a bright future in the infant Jesus, the Light of the World and Prince of Peace.

For each of the twelve days of Christmas you will find:

- a short **reading** from the Bible to read and meditate on;
- a **reflection** to help us to see the Christmas story afresh;
- a **challenge** inviting us to consider what being calm and bright means within the story of our own lives today;
- finally, a **prayer** as we treasure this story in our hearts and seek to shine as a light in the world around us.

Sammi Tooze Discipleship Adviser, Diocese of York

Contents

Good news of great joy

| **Read** Luke 2.8-12

"Do not be afraid; for see – I am bringing you good news of great joy for all the people ... "

Reading or hearing endless headlines about war, natural disasters and violence is so wearing. Do you ever, like me, feel a need for some positive stories?

Recently, I discovered the Good News Network online which has helped to redress the balance. It's been heartening to notice that most features come from people's ordinary, everyday lives, rather than from events or people in the media spotlight. In many of the stories, we encounter God in the ordinariness of everyday life.

In today's reading we meet the first witnesses to the birth of Jesus: shepherds, disturbed during their night-watch by angels. They never questioned whether they were good enough or important enough – this good news was, and is, for all people. Perhaps the shepherds had understandable fear to begin with, but the angels' message is to be calm, rather than afraid, and to focus on the brightness of the good news proclaimed to them.

Today, like at that first Christmas, there is calm as God enters into our world with peace and humility. And there is also joy as brightness shines out of the ordinariness of everyday life. As we journey together through this Christmas season, we too inhabit that peace and that joy as we give thanks for the good news passed down to us through the ages from those ordinary shepherds.

> Spend some time this Christmas Day giving thanks for the good news in your life – and praying for calm where there is fear or hurt.

Lord Jesus Christ
your birth at Bethlehem
draws us to kneel in wonder at heaven touching earth:
accept our heartfelt praise as we worship you,
our Saviour and our God.
Amen.

Stories of the saints

Read Romans 1.9-12

"I remember you always in my prayers ...
that we may be mutually encouraged by
each other's faith, both yours and mine."

Who most inspires you?

It might be someone well-known, or someone known to
you – a writer, an artist or a musician, an activist, a religious
or political leader – contemporary or historical.

I've often been inspired by people who have shown
humility and compassion in their lives. I also love reading
about people of faith who in some cases died centuries
ago – yet we remember them and how they lived their lives.

The Church of England's calendar of saints provides a helpful framework for recalling stories of people who have gone before us. Today on 26 December, for example, we remember Stephen, the first Christian martyr, whose story is recorded in the Acts of the Apostles. These are stories of discipleship, stories which tell of their humanity in all their flaws as well as their strengths.

As Paul writes in today's reading, their stories spiritually strengthen us and encourage our faith. We hear their stories and we can be inspired by them – they shine bright to us, pointing beyond themselves and their way of life to the glory of God. They influence us in how we shape our own lives of faith today.

So, as we reflect on the faith of the saints this Christmas, may we too shine as today's storytellers for the next generation.

> Spend some time recalling the story of someone who has inspired you in your life and faith, and give thanks for them.

God of holiness,
your glory is proclaimed in every age:
as we rejoice in the faith of your saints,
inspire us to follow their example
with boldness and joy.
Amen.

Holy faces, holy people

Read 2 Corinthians 3.17-18
"And all of us ... seeing the glory of the Lord as though reflected in a mirror ... are being transformed ... "

It's not everyone's favourite part of going to church, but for me, the moment where we share the peace always has a profound impact.

Worship lies at the heart of who we are as Christians – in worship we encounter God and are changed, becoming more the people God creates us to be. When we share the peace, we meet with Christ in the face of one another, "seeing the glory of the Lord as though reflected in a mirror" as Paul describes it in today's reading. I really admire churches who take their time over this, recognising that we are God's holy people from whom the light of Christ shines brightly.

Of course, this idealistic picture of holiness is not always the case. As human beings we are challenged by impatience, frustrations, annoying habits – the image of complete peace and perfection isn't often the reality of day-to-day living. But God creates us to be perfectly imperfect, and holiness finds itself right in the middle of that as we live in community with other people.

As we give thanks for the birth of Jesus among us, let us remember God with us, God's image within us and in the face of one another, mirroring the light of Christ in our relationships with others day by day.

> Think about the people you will see this week, and what you see of God's image reflected through them.

O God, our light and our salvation,
illuminate our lives,
that we may see your goodness
in the land of the living,
and, looking on your beauty,
may be changed into the likeness
of Jesus Christ our Lord. Amen.

Praising God and singing

Read Luke 2.13-14

"And suddenly there was with the angel a multitude of the heavenly host, praising God ... "

If I asked you what your favourite song was, what would it be?

I would definitely struggle to name just one, I have so many! I have several playlists of my favourite music: playlists of feel-good songs, cheesy Christmas music, film soundtracks, and even one of my favourite carols which I like playing very loudly in my car!

Singing is good for our souls. Scientific research shows singing to be good for our physical health, emotional wellbeing, and brain development. It calms and centres us. Whether you are part of a church community or not, Christmas hymns or carols are well-known to many of us, because singing them is part of our culture. I wonder how much we think about the words we're singing, though? Singing carols is a form of storytelling – we are singing our story of faith, and we are formed and shaped by the words we express.

During Advent and Christmas, we sing of the story of God with us, and how we find our own story within that miracle. So, as we continue to sing the Christmas story, let us reflect on the words as we join with the angels from that first Christmas night in praising God – and singing.

> Spend some time listening to or singing a favourite carol – perhaps one you've not heard this year – and pondering the story it tells.

Give us the music of your praise, O God,
morning, noon and night,
that our lives may join
in your dance of holy light,
and our lips never cease
in singing glory to your name.
Amen.

Joy in gentleness

Read Philippians 4.4-7

"Rejoice in the Lord always; and again I will say, Rejoice. Let your gentleness be known to everyone."

I've never been one for telling jokes.

Many years ago, I used to think that I was a boring person for not joining in quoting from sit coms or making people laugh. But in time I came to realize that joy doesn't always have to be extroverted, loud or exuberant – that being an introvert and on the quieter end of life's spectrum, I could still encounter joy.

Since then, I've thought of joy more like an inner glow, something we experience much more deeply than a service-level happiness. It's one of the reasons I love Midnight Mass. There's something so moving about worshipping under the cover of darkness, and the gentleness in that joyful expectation.

In today's reading, Paul very clearly holds joy and gentleness together. Gentleness is offered as a way that joy is expressed. We experience so much of this gentle rejoicing in everyday life – in a hug from someone we love, in cradling a warm cup of tea, in practising gratitude, and in being kind to ourselves and to others.

Jesus' gentleness is known to us as he is born among us, and so our gentleness is now known to the world as people made in the image of God. We can live and embody that gentleness as joy-filled people of God.

> What comes to mind when you think of rejoicing? Where have you experienced the gentleness of joy this week?

Give to us, Lord Christ,
the fullness of grace,
your presence and your very self,
for you are our portion and our delight,
now and for ever.
Amen.

Rest for our minds

Read Matthew 11.28-30

Jesus said, "Come to me, all you that are weary and are carrying heavy burdens, and I will give you rest ... "

A friend of mine recently downloaded an app on her phone that identifies the birds she can hear singing around her.

After using it for a few weeks, she realised it was encouraging her to be more attentive to birdsong and more in tune with God's creation. For her, this spiritual attentiveness was deeply linked with mental rest and wellbeing.

Our contemporary culture is so demanding – whether it's the craving of immediate replies to messages, buying the next new exciting bit of technology, or the pressure of complex family lives. By taking time to listen to birdsong, my friend was noticing that her mental rest was just as important as physical rest. Being able to take time to rest our minds offers a sense of restoration and recreation, enabling us to recharge. We can take time simply to be the people God creates us to be.

Today's reading reminds us that Jesus knows we need – and offers us – the gift of rest. Meditating on Jesus' invitation offers us space to think about what mental rest we might need. It might mean putting our phones down, turning the TV off, having an email sabbath, and simply enjoying resting in the presence of God.

> Give time today to something that will help you embrace God's heavenly peace.

O God of holiness,
you create all things in your image;
help us to receive your recreative power of rest,
that our minds may be renewed
in your heavenly peace.
Amen.

Rest for our souls

Read Hebrews 4.9-11a

" ... a sabbath rest still remains for the people of God."

I have gained a reputation in my office. Having gently encouraged colleagues to take their lunch breaks away from their desks, people now apologise for working through lunch even when I'm not there!

Establishing patterns of rest-taking is partly about physical and mental health, and also part of who we are as God's people. As today's reading from Hebrews reminds us, as people made in God's image, we need to follow the pattern God established on the seventh day of creation and "also cease from [our] labours as God did from his". Christmas might not always seem very restful, although perhaps rest is something that we're not good at year round, not least within the Church. I have heard so often of people who have been too busy to take their day off, or have too much to do to be able to spend an evening enjoying time for themselves.

Sabbath is a spiritual gift. As well as being about rest, it's also about setting aside time for things that bring us joy. Perhaps as we enter into a new year, it can be a shared resolution to encourage one another in breaking down barriers of guilt, to enable healthy, joyful, restorative sabbath rest in God.

> Set some time aside this week for yourself, perhaps making space for something that brings you joy.

Eternal God,
as we enter into a new year,
calm and quieten our souls;
keep us humble and full of wonder
and trusting as we live in your love;
through Jesus Christ our Lord.
Amen.

Day 8

New Year's Day

Rhythms of life

Read Luke 10.38-42

"Martha had a sister named Mary, who sat at the Lord's feet."

Having never been much interested in New Year Resolutions, last year I set myself a challenge to cook one new recipe every month in 2024.

I am proud – and still slightly surprised – to say that I succeeded!

New Year's Resolutions come from a place of simultaneously looking back and looking forwards; of reflecting on what's important to us, and how we want that to shape how we live.

We might call this a rhythm of life: a way to find a balance between "being" and "doing". In the story of Mary and Martha, we see Jesus upholding Mary, who has chosen to stop busying herself with tasks (doing), and instead sits at Jesus' feet (being).

A rhythm of life is not a set of binding rules, but finding creative and flexible frameworks for living our everyday faith. Exploring our own way of life encourages us to think about where our places of stillness are, how we pray, how we seek after justice, and how we share our faith with others.

In beginning this new year, perhaps we can consider what our own way of life looks like – taking time to sit at Jesus' feet, listening to and being shaped by God's living way.

> Reflect on what your way of life looks like. What is God calling you to do – to be?

Lord Christ,
as we sit at your infant feet,
teach us your living way;
for you are our Word and Wisdom,
one God in three,
now and for ever.
Amen.

Beauty in silence

Read Luke 2.15-20

"But Mary treasured all these words and pondered them in her heart."

There is a contradiction in many of our well-known Christmas music: where some speak of silence, and others speak of rejoicing in song.

On one hand, we have "O little town of Bethlehem, how still we see thee lie!"; on the other we have "Hark! the herald angels sing". I don't however think that one cannot exist in preference to the other.

In today's reading from Luke's Gospel we are given a wonderful example in Mary. At the birth of Jesus, as the shepherds and angels rejoice in creating lots of noise,

Mary chooses instead to contemplate and to rejoice in silence. Mary models for us a calm, contemplative way of approaching Christmas, and the whole of life beyond the season.

The practice of silence can be challenging in our noisy, busy, distracting world. But silence has been a central part to many Christian communities for centuries.

Silence enables us to encounter God, to rejoice in prayer as listening before we speak. Silence allows us to discover something of God in quite a different way to when there is plenty of noise around. We enter into a particular kind of holiness where our souls are open to the transformative peace of God.

Spend some time today in silence, allowing your heart to rejoice calmly in God as Mary's did that first Christmas.

O God of peace,
on whom our souls wait in silence;
renew in our hearts an inner stillness,
as we seek to treasure
your Word made flesh
in Jesus Christ our Lord.
Amen.

Love's pure light

Read John 1.6-9

"The true light, which enlightens everyone, was coming into the world."

There is a tradition in my home on the First Sunday of Advent – in the afternoon I head over to York Minster to sing in the Advent Procession, and afterwards I return home to put up my Christmas decorations.

There is always a slightly anxious moment of untangling fairy lights, holding my breath and hoping they still work! Lighting up our homes at Christmas is a tradition which has spilled over into secular culture. The first Christmas trees to arrive in the UK in the nineteenth-century were decorated with candles to symbolise Jesus as the light of the world. Before very long, electric Christmas lights began to become very fashionable across the country.

It's an appealing thought that the fairy lights we see so often – even beyond Christmas – are not only there to look pretty. They are there as a symbol of Love's Pure Light. In today's reading, we hear about John the Baptist, who is also described as a symbol – or a witness – to the light. God had called him to a life which testified to the true light which was coming into the world, in the birth of Jesus.

God is love, and Jesus is the light of that love who has come into the world. As with John the Baptist, and with Christmas lights, it is now our calling to shine as we witness in love to the Pure Light of Jesus.

Think about one thing you could do today to share God's love with someone you know.

Lord Jesus, Light from Light,
you have come among us.
Help us who live by your light
to shine as lights in your world.
Amen.

Even darkness

Read Psalm 139.6-11
"Even darkness is no darkness with you ...
darkness and light to you are both alike."

**Starlight is so mesmerising and beautiful.
There's something very moving about looking
upwards on a calm, still night, working out how
many tiny dots we can see above.**

Light is a powerful symbol in the Christian tradition,
particularly at Christmas when we welcome Christ as the
light that shines in darkness. However, it's important not
to fall into the trap of associating only light with God and
all that is good, and only darkness with all that is bad
or difficult.

Today's reading from Psalm 139 is a helpful reminder that to God "darkness and light are both alike". In other words, light and darkness exist in balance, and God is present no matter what part of that spectrum we experience. As a night-owl, I actually experience something very calming as the sun sets and the darkness of night descends.

The Psalmist challenges the worldly perception of darkness as a purely negative space to avoid. So many key biblical events take place in darkness. Jesus' birth is proclaimed to the shepherds at night. The Magi travel because they have observed his star at night. And, or course, Jesus' resurrection occurs before dawn on Easter Day.

As we experience the darker days of winter, we have the opportunity to reframe our view of darkness, and discover our own epiphany of the presence of God, to whom the darkness and the light are both alike.

> Spend some time today – tonight – meditating on God's presence in the darkness as well as in the light.

In the darkness of unknowing,
and in the light of peace,
draw near to us, O God,
in Christ, our Redeemer and our Lord.
Amen.

Shine as a light in the world

> **Read** Matthew 5.14-16
> Jesus said to the crowds, "You are the light of the world ... let your light shine before others ... "

How long do you keep your Christmas decorations up? I always keep mine up until Epiphany. It would be a shame for the wise men to have travelled so far, only to discover that they'd missed the party!

The season of Epiphany invites us to revisit three key moments in Jesus' life when his glory is revealed: the visit of the Magi, the first miracle at Cana and the moment

Jesus is proclaimed as God's beloved Son at his baptism. Whenever a baptism takes place today, the newly baptised are given a candle at the end of the service and invited to "Shine as a light in the world".

As people of God, we are being sent out into the world to love, to witness, and to shine, as Jesus invites his first hearers to do in today's reading. We are called to be calm and bright all year round.

In baptism we are called to love and trust in God, to love our neighbour as ourselves, and seek peace and justice – this is how we can shine as God's light. We shine brightly as we become a blessing to others and make a difference in the world around us. We help other people to see what God is like, simply by being the people God creates us to be.

> Think about what your everyday faith looks like. How can you enable God's light to shine through you in the week – and the year – ahead?

O God,
who led the wise men by the shining of a star
to find the Christ, the Light from light,
lead us in our earthly pilgrimage,
and embolden us to shine your light in the world.
Amen.

Next Steps

Jesus Christ is at the heart of our vision for the Church of England. Where will a life centred on Christ take you?

We hope you have enjoyed these #FollowTheStar reflections.

Here are some possible next steps on your journey:

- **Connect with God all year round with the Everyday Faith app.** Journey daily with reflections like those in this booklet to inspire, equip and encourage you in your everyday faith. The app is free to download for iOS and Android via **cofe.io/EverydayFaithApp**

- **Join with others in worship and service at your local church.** Find thousands of services and events, groups and activities taking place both on site and online all year round via **AChurchNearYou.com**

- **Explore baptism for yourself or for your child.** Find out more about being baptised and how you or your child can take this important first step on the amazing journey of Christian faith at **churchofengland.org/christenings**

- **Build prayer into your day using the Daily Prayer app with audio.** Visit **cofe.io/DailyPrayer** to join hundreds of thousands of people who have found daily calm and inspiration by making these services part of their rhythm of life.

Published 2024 by Church House Publishing
www.chpublishing.co.uk

Church House Publishing, Church House, Great Smith Street,
London SW1P 3AZ

© The Archbishops' Council of the Church of England 2024

ISBN 978 1 78140 490 4 (Single Copy)
ISBN 978 1 78140 491 1 (10-Pack)
ISBN 978 1 78140 492 8 (50-Pack)
ISBN 978 1 78140 493 5 (LARGE PRINT)

Except for quotations from the psalms, Scripture quotations are
from the New Revised Standard Version of the Bible, Anglicized
Edition, copyright © 1989, 1995 by the Division of Christian Education
of the National Council of the Churches of Christ in the USA. Used
by permission. All rights reserved.

Material from *Common Worship: Services and Prayers for the Church
of England* included here (including psalm quotations, psalm prayers,
Collects) is copyright © The Archbishops' Council 2000-2008 and
used here with permission.

The opinions expressed in this book are those of the author.

All rights reserved. No part of this publication may be copied
reproduced or stored or transmitted without written permission from
copyright@churchofengland.org

Design and typesetting by www.penguinboy.net
Photo on page 6: Greg Milner
Printed in the UK Core Publications Ltd, Kettering

> "Our prayer is that all of us ... may find this
> moment of hope-filled and joyful calm as
> we worship together this Christmas."
> ARCHBISHOPS JUSTIN WELBY
> AND STEPHEN COTTRELL

Follow The Star – Calm and Bright invites you to dwell
in the still centre of the Christmas story where, in the
words of Silent Night, "All is calm, all is bright ... "

For each of the twelve days of Christmas, this booklet
offers a short **reading** from the Bible, a **reflection** to
help you see the Christmas story afresh; a **challenge**
inviting you to consider what being calm and bright
means within the story of your own life, and a **prayer**
to help you treasure the story in your heart.

Follow The Star – Calm and Bright is the Church of England's theme
for Advent and Christmas 2024. These reflections have been written by
Sammi Tooze, Discipleship Adviser for the Diocese of York.

You're very welcome at a church near you this Advent
and Christmas. Find your nearest services and events
and get involved via **AChurchNearYou.com**

*Available individually, in packs
of 10 or 50, and in LARGE PRINT*

ISBN: 978-1-78140-490-4

CHURCH HOUSE
PUBLISHING
www.chpublishing.co.uk

9 781781 404904